CHANGE *your* LANGUAGE
CHANGE *your* LIFE

Exploring What You Can Say Differently Today
To Change Your Tomorrow!

JOTINA BUCK

CHANGE YOUR LANGUAGE...CHANGE YOUR LIFE
Exploring What You Can Say Differently Today to Change Your Tomorrow!
By Jotina Buck

DEDICATION

I dedicate this book to my parents, the late Rev. James & Sharon Buck, in memoriam. Your unwavering faith and love towards humanity shaped my life. Since your transition I have been inspired even more to share love, practice gratitude, and be kind. Thanks for instilling Godly values in me and rearing me to be a bold God-fearing woman. It is my prayer to celebrate your lives & legacies through the life I live. I love you Momma & Daddy.

ACKNOWLEDGMENTS

I acknowledge that I am absolutely nothing without God. I am extremely grateful that He chooses to use me to share His message of hope and love in the world. It is my sincere hope to be continuous love and light in the darkest places. I pray that this book is used to bring Him glory.

To my best girl, Lauryn Vickers, thanks for sharing mommy with the world. Thanks for being selfless and a constant example of the purest form of love. You inspire me to be better. It is my prayer that you are inspired by God's work through me and you carry this legacy on forever.

To my big sister and little brother, Chantaye & Quincy, your support, love, and encouragement has carried me many days. Thanks for investing in this project and believing in me. I love you two to pieces!

To my ace, Share Johnson, your friendship, love, and support is valuable and cannot be compared. Your candid critiques and depth of knowledge on any subject matter has challenged me to dig deeper even when I thought there was no more. Thanks for being the reflection of true friendship. I love you chic.

To my team, Robin, Christy, Jamesha, Jacarolyn, Mark Doze, and Mahogany…thanks for helping take my brand to the next level. Your countless hours & never ending efforts are truly appreciated. Each of you are experts in your respective areas and I know my business will never be the same as a result of your expertise.

To Ramone & Verily Harper and the entire BNB Consulting staff, thanks for interpreting this vision and helping me birth Change Your Language,

Change Your Life. You all were always available at the drop of a hat and never withheld giving your highest service. It is such a pleasure to do business with people I know I can call friends & family forever. I love you two.

To my Pastor, Dr. Timothy W. Sloan, thanks for shaping the message, mission, and movement of Change Your Language, Change Your Life. I will never forget the Think Big sermon series. I felt that series was a direct challenge tailored for me. I took those scriptures and dissected each of them carefully. What do you know? Here I am now basking in the manifestation of my courage to Think Big. I love you to life.

To Dr. Sonya Sloan, you are more than a first lady. You have been a mentor, confidant, and soul guide for me throughout this journey. I could go on and on about how much you've blessed me but I will just say....you changed my life forever! You are indeed genius. Joining your women's business development program; Great Minds Think Alike was the best decision of my life. Thanks for availing yourself. I love you "First"!

To Kim Bady, thanks for being there from conception to manifestation of Change Your Language, Change Your Life. You are the best sister-friend a girl could ask for. Your mentorship has helped me increase in business and in spirit. Thanks for being an authentic soul and always being the same. Love you Kimmie!

To Betty Landers and Nell Walder, thanks for always praying for me. I know there were times when you all were praying specifically for me. I love both of you. My Divine Prayer Warriors!

To Anthony Riley and Chad Brawley, thanks for being available to critique and share advice. Thanks for always sharing in my career highlights and for being men of standard. You guys are really my brothers and I love you both.

To Karenda Smith "Queen of Styling", thanks for capturing the perfect image for the cover. Your work is always excellent and captures the true essence of who I am at the core.

To Germaine Compton, of Tushea Productions, thanks for designing a stellar cover. Your work is impeccable.

To Deana Marshall, of Article Write Up, thanks for editing this literary piece and helping to ensure my vision was articulated precisely.

To every person who took time to listen to the vision, share in highlights along the way, pray when needed, and celebrate during great victory.... Thanks! I know that without all of my family, friends, sister-friends, and major supporters I would not be here. Please note, your support carries me. If I were to start listing names I am certain it would be another book. I just want to say, I could not have gotten this far without your support, prayers, encouragement, and unwavering love. I love you all!

30 CHAPTERS OF ENLIGHTENMENT'S

FOREWORD

By Sonya M. Sloan, M.D.

Motivating and Empowering words to live by: Change your Language, Change your Life! This is a book you can't afford not to have in your arsenal of "Self-Help!" Ms. Jotina Buck has captured and tailored the perfect words to inspire every walk of life to not only revamp your vocabulary but your entire outlook on how to live day-to-day successfully! Her words, translated and encouraged by her own REAL life experiences and above all-odds challenges, exude the very premise of how one can truly speak life into themselves and succeed at nearly anything!

Jotina's passion to teach and help others transcends boundaries of gender, race or religion. Ms. Buck is a REAL student of life. She is a believer of living out loud and on purpose. Her vast knowledge and experiences shared throughout her book creates moments of vulnerable transparency while paying it forward to help others excel at their own calling and passion in life.

If life is really about relationships, then I have been honored to be in the midst of a woman who knows how to overcome adversity and use it not only for her own good, but yours as well…all through the POWER of WORDS! So what are you saying to yourself? Per Ms. Jotina Buck, Change your language and you CAN and WILL change your life!

PREFACE

We are all familiar with the saying, "You are what you eat." Through this transparent literary piece, I want to infect you with an even more powerful saying, "You are what you think and say." One of the greatest truths in life is that it flows from the inside out. We are affected by what happens inside through our feelings and thoughts. This in turn affects our emotions, the words we speak, and the actions we choose to take. What you choose to own as feelings is ultimately up to you. Change your Language and You Change your Life. If you want to scale the mountain of life with passion and reach the pinnacle of human potential on the highest peak, then take charge of your thoughts and become the CEO of your life.

Easier said than done, right? This book focuses on how to change your language, recognize and declare God's promises, foster life-enhancing habits, and make an agreement with yourself to enrich your life by following through on what you say you want to do or accomplish.

"To meet the great tasks that are before us, we require all our intelligence, and we must be sound and wholesome in mind. We must proceed in order. The price of anger is failure." *~Elwood Hendricks*

I AM

I tell myself 'I AM GREAT' every day because every day
the world says something different.
I tell myself 'I AM STRONG' every day because every day
the world says something different.
I tell myself 'I AM BEAUTIFUL' every day because every day
the world says something different.
I tell myself 'I AM BRILLIANT' every day because every day
the world says something different.
I tell myself 'I AM LIGHT' every day because every day
the world says something different.
I tell myself 'I AM LOVE' every day because every day
the world says something different.
I tell myself 'I AM POWER' every day because every day
the world says something different.
I tell myself 'I AM PEACE' every day because every day
the world says something different.
I tell myself 'I AM SUCCESS' every day because every day
the world says something different.
I don't try to stand out, I just do.
I don't try to be, I just be.
I don't say I will be, I JUST AM.
I AM because HE IS and that's enough.
I AM ENOUGH.

Jotina Buck

INTRODUCTION

'Change Your Language, Change Your Life' encompasses spiritual truths, personal experiences, and powerful prayers that can be applied to these five areas of your life or whatever area you wish to change: Spirituality, Health, Wealth, Happiness, and Relationships. To implement these principles, the following methods/tools are used: Visualization, Meditation, Affirmation, and Balance. *'Change Your Language Change Your Life'* is a unique literary work in that you too become a part of it. It will evoke tears, laughter, reflection, action, forgiveness, healing, creativity, knowledge, growth, and ultimately challenge you to LIVE! This is not your typical book from the average shelf. This piece is an all-encompassing tool to get "the work" done! It is a book, a journal, a devotional, and even a memoir.

There are four major principles of life-change; Spirituality, Focus, Balance, and Gratitude. Throughout this book, I will share 30 Enlightenment's to Unlock Unlimited Possibilities. You will read personal stories and enlightenment's hinged on these four principles and more about each of these major principles and how they can and will change your life direction. Use the space after each chapter to write down new thoughts about the way you want your life to be. You will develop new patterns of thinking. Changes will start to happen and positive thoughts will start to enter your mind. Act on them immediately and believe in your new reality. The results will change your life.

In the space provided you can write from your very soul about what you think and feel without being judged by anyone. Your writings are secure, so relax and let go. When you commit something to paper, somehow it takes on a deeper meaning and permanency in your life. So write easy and freely with no restrictions or limitations. Visualize what could be and make it your new reality. Expect to walk away with increased energy, meditation skills, prayers of faith and affirmation, tips to healthy living, and other tools that will catapult you to increased levels in your life.

CHAPTER 1

LIFE CHANGER

I want to share a short story of inspiration with you. On August 20, 2002, I was eager about going off to college. My family and friends were prepared for the big send off too. The night before I had spoken with my daddy and he assured me that the truck was packed and ready to go to Prairie View A & M University. The morning of the 20th I awoke to my mother's house dress in the middle of the floor and the burglar bars on the door locked. I was locked in the house. The room felt cold and I was clueless as to why I wasn't headed off to school excitedly with my parents. (Note: Although my mother and father were separated during this time, they were very cordial to each other. My father lived in our childhood home while my mother and I stayed in an apartment.) Well my mother was not at the apartment with me and I was home alone. Feeling scared and extremely puzzled, I picked up the phone and began to call my mother. With getting no answer I tried calling my sister and then brother – again with no answer from either. I no sooner hung up the phone bewildered to what was going on and suddenly the phone rang. It was my brother in law. All I could hear was my sister's horrid screams in the background. I demanded he tell me what was going on. He slowly broke the news. My daddy suffered a heart attack and was found dead in his home. This was the beginning of what should have been a memorable journey yet it appeared to be a nightmare. Hence, I began my freshmen year of college burying my daddy. August 20th is a day I'll never forget.

Fast forward to June 8, 2009, the Summer of my senior year of college; seven years later. Clearly, I did not sail through college in four years. On June 8,

2009, like clockwork, I called my mom to see what was for lunch. There was this place by her house that sold barbeque oxtails and boy were they good. I asked her what time did they open. She responded, "11:30." I told her I would come to her house for lunch and quickly got off of the phone. I worked in childcare and I could not talk on the phone while I had my students. We exchanged our verbal love and hung up. Exactly 18 minutes later she was calling me back. Before I answered I said to myself, "I just told her I can't talk. What is it?" As I answered the phone I quickly noticed it wasn't my mother's voice on the other line. It was her neighbor. She asked in a faint and shaky voice. Do you know the lady that lives at 8409 Westcott?" I replied, "Yes Why?" She responded, "I think she's dying." I immediately dropped the phone and ran to my supervisor. Hysterical, I could not drive. My boss drove me to my mom's house. As we turned the corner, cars filled the street. The ambulance and first responders kept us all back while they worked to resuscitate my mom. They were able to get a pulse after about 45 minutes. They rushed her to the hospital. For four days I slept on the cold floor of Lyndon B. Johnson Hospital. I refused to leave my mother's side. After all, I am the baby of my family and I was the very last child still living with my mother. We were more than mother-daughter. We were best friends. I revered her and I felt she valued me the same. I shared my secrets with her and she kept them near never forsaking me. On June 11th, 2009 at about 8:25 pm my mother transitioned to be with Our Heavenly Father. This was the point where I felt I could not go on. I remember sinking into this deep depression. I was like the vampire girl. I would sleep all day. I wanted it dark and I would eat until I felt better. Every day I would rehearse this story over and over again. I would ask myself the question, "Why me?" I complained about how horrible my life was. Most times, I rejected invites from my friends because I did not want to be subjected to seeing them with their parents. There was a spirit of sorrow, enviousness, jealousy, and unbearable grief birthing in me.

Little did I know that I was breeding negativity in my mind each time I complained, rehearsed my story, or replayed those horrific events. I never thought I could come out of the place of saying, "Why did I have to lose both of my parents before the age of 25?" I was dying on the inside and I didn't even realize it. I was speaking defeat over my life and allowing this tragedy to dominate my life in a negative way.

In early 2010 a girlfriend asked me to create a vision board with her. As I sat down to create this vision board I didn't know what to expect. One thing I was sure of is that if I continued in the manner I had been carrying on, the turnout could not be good. I took my friend up on that offer and created a vision board. I am not sure I was completely aware of what was happening neurologically while creating this board but when I look in retrospect I know it was divine. I placed words such as peace, love, hope, and freedom alongside my personal goals for my life. I reluctantly placed this board on the wall in my front room. As I passed by it each day, I can honestly say I felt hope and determination grow inside of me. I eventually started to repeat the words that were on my vision board. I used this board as a point of reference for the dark and cloudy days. I would repeat my goals and dreams aloud. Creating my vision board is what defined the pivot in my life. Speaking words of hope, love, peace, freedom, and joy helped me talk myself to a place of healing, wholeness and restoration.

Why Creative Visioning is important?

90% of what our brain processes is visual. Many of our subconscious thoughts and desires are stored in the creative, visual areas of our brain. We normally don't access them because we filter them in various ways, but when making a vision board, your brain will reveal 'blind spots' and desires that have not yet had the opportunity to come to your awareness.

A vision board is a collage of images, inspirational maps and words of your dreams, goals and aspirations. Vision boards serve as a visual reminder of your goals, dreams, and aspirations. The Universe responds to what we believe about our lives and the world around us. All that we desire is in the Universe and we have the full capacity to manifest our desires.

Our minds can hold about seven pieces of information at one time. Yet there are millions of pieces of information available to us at every moment. So, to ensure you don't get overwhelmed, our minds learns to filter information and to only show you pieces of information it thinks is relevant. This is one of the key ways that vision boards work. The very act of creating the vision board tells our mind what's important and it just may draw your attention to something you might not otherwise have noticed.

So often we have the most amazing ideas, dreams and visions but sometimes our plans are only half realized. If we don't capture key ingredients before they are forgotten or overlooked, our visions won't reach their full potential.

How to Create a Vision Board in 5 Steps

Step 1: Go through magazines and tear inspirational images out. No gluing yet. Just let yourself have lots of fun looking through magazines and pulling out pictures, words, or headlines that strike your attention. Make a big pile.

Step 2: Go through the images and begin to lay your favorites on the board. Eliminate any images that no longer feel right or fit your overall vision. This step is where your genuine desires and intuition comes in. As you lay out pictures start creating a theme and sense of how your board will be laid out. For example, you might assign a theme to each corner of the board. You may just want images all over your board. You might want to fold the board into quads to tell a story.

Step 3: Glue everything onto the board. Add writing if you want. You can draw, paint, or write words with markers.

Step 4: This step is optional but very powerful. Leave space in the middle to add a vibrant, happy, and radiant photo of yourself. This helps with seeing yourself in the future with your desires manifested.

Step 5: Hang your vision board in a place where you will see it often.

Tips for an Appealing Vision Board

- Use vibrant colors. Your vision board should captivate your attention daily.

- Think Limitless. Let your mind run free and dream.

- Look for the unfamiliar. Get outside of your normal box.

- Add personal affirmations. Make you board personalized for your desires.

- Work to create what inspires you and not just an artistic masterpiece.

"Without leaps of imagination, or dreaming, we lose the excitement of possibilities. Dreaming, after all, is a form of planning." Gloria Steinem

When was the last time you noticed yourself speaking negativity into your life? Write down the words that you used and then write down a positive word to replace it. In addition, come up with 10 positive words that you don't already use in your everyday communications to yourself or others. Plan on adding them to your daily vocabulary. If you haven't yet ever created a vision board, I challenge you today to start one.

_____

_____

_____

_____

_____

_____

_____

_____

_____

_____

_____

_____

_____

CHAPTER 2

THE POWER OF YOUR WORDS

The language we use shapes our lives. The old cliché suggests God gave us two ears and one mouth to listen more and speak less. Destructive speaking does not help anyone. I understand at times we have to speak out about negative things however, even then it can be articulated with grace. The Bible in the book of James chapter three speaks much about the power of the tongue. It declares that anyone who is able to control their tongue is a perfect person. It illustrates the power of the tongue by comparing it to a small rudder that directs a large ship. God declares in the bible that life and death are in the power of the tongue. Death and life are in the power of the tongue, and they who indulge in it shall eat the fruit of it. (Proverbs 18: 21) When negative thoughts are formed in our mind and in our heart of feelings it is often wise to speak positively instead of succumbing to the negative.

Language plays a very significant role in influencing our life and the real spirit of who we are. As far-fetched as it may sound, but true, our language defines our happiness proportion and the quality of our life. And by just changing our language, there is a huge shift that can be invited into our life.

The first and most imperative question that we can ask ourselves is 'how can language define happiness in our life'? The statements that we make about ourselves and life define what we think about it. So, if we think and say negative things about ourselves and our life, the negative belief is reinforced in the mind and our mind starts to operate from that negative belief. If there are negative thoughts and emotions in our mind all the time, we will constantly feel burdened, stressed and sad.

Likewise, if we have a positive and motivating language all the time, our mind becomes programmed to think positive and thus we feel happier and our life is fulfilled.

What is your language?

First step in bringing a positive change in your language is to observe it. Is your conversation negative or positive? Do most of your sentences have negations like no, not, never, etc.? Do you find yourself talking about what is not right in your life or around you? Do you often complain about all the things wrong with the world? If the answers to most of these questions are in affirmative, you are making sure that happiness doesn't come anywhere near you. If that is what your life plan includes, then you are on track! But if you want to live a happy and joyous life, it is time for you to revise your language skills!

Change your vocabulary

One of the most important things that you can do to change your language for the good, is to change your vocabulary. Give a thought on the most common words used by you and see what type of words are they. Does your "favorite word basket" have more negative words than positive? Do words like stress, painful, anger, busy, and sad play a dominating role in your sentences? If the answers to most of these questions end in a "yes" for you, then it is time for you to obtain a new dictionary and learn words that speak life! It is very important to change the words you use. Some simple tips and examples are: Instead of using the word 'problem' you can say 'challenge'. The word "problem" brings with it a connotation which expresses that something cannot be solved. Challenge on the other hand is something difficult but achievable.

Change your statements

Another important tip is to change your usual statements. For example, if you have a habit of saying, "I don't want to be late", change it to 'I am always on time'. Similarly, shift from saying, "I don't want to be sick." to "I am healthy and fit." The basic rule here is to focus on what you want rather than what you do not want. What you want will be affirmed important and will receive the attention in your life and not the unwanted stuff.

Never complete a negative statement

In the beginning, changing your language habits may seem a bit challenging; however, awareness and commitment can help you turn it around. The most important step is to pay attention to what you are saying, whether in your mind to yourself or to others. The moment you find yourself starting a negative statement, stop then and there. Start a new habit: never complete your negative statements.

Once you stop in the midst of these negative statements, your mind intercepts the message clearly that you don't want to use those negative sentences. Then slowly you will find that you use those negative sentences even less.

No complaints

Remove all complaints from your daily conversations. Complaints are those negative programs in your language that reiterate what all is wrong with you and with the world. This kind of a program operates as a vicious cycle. The more complaints you make, the worse you feel, the worse you feel the more complaints you make and it just goes on and on. Instead, be brave and take complaints out of your conversations and replace it with words that express your thankfulness. Rather than talking about what is not right in your life, start talking about what is right. For starters you can kick off by thanking God for the unlimited oxygen you get every day, free of charge.

No justifications

Stop giving justifications so much space and effort in your conversations. Stop using words and phrases such as "because" and "that is why". These words give lame reasons for you doing or not doing something. Those justifications are actually unnecessary. You can and you should do what you want without any compulsion of giving a good reason for it. Add these few subtle changes to your language and see how it transforms your life in a big way. Once you make these changes in your language, your mind will receive the message that you have shifted from a negative state to a positive one. Thus, the mind will help you to stay happy now that it knows that is what you want. Change your language to change your life!

List 20 adjectives that describe you. Now read through them. Are they all positive? If not, why? What can you do to turn them from a negative to a positive? Make a plan to start changing them today.

_____

_____

_____

_____

_____

_____

_____

_____

_____

_____

_____

_____

_____

_____

_____

_____

_____

_____

CHAPTER 3

SPIRITUALITY

As mentioned in the introduction, spirituality is one of the 4 major principles in life change. One of the great gifts of spiritual knowledge is that it calibrates your sense of self to reveal something you may not have ever imagined was within you. Spirituality says that even if you think you're limited and small, it simply isn't so. You're greater and more powerful than you have ever imagined. A great and divine light exists inside of you. This same light is also in everyone you know and in everyone you will ever know in the future. You may think you're limited to just your physical body and state of affairs — including your gender, race, family, job, and status in life — but spirituality comes in and says "There is more than this."

Notice that the word 'spirit' is synonymous with words like inspire and expire. This is especially appropriate because when you're filled with spiritual energy you feel great inspiration, and when the spiritual life force leaves your body, your time on this earth expires. These are two of the main themes of the spiritual journey:

- Allowing yourself to be filled with inspiration, which also translates into love, joy, wisdom, peacefulness, and service.

- Remembering that an inevitable expiration awaits you; ready to take you away from the very circumstances you may think are so very important right now.

The study of spirituality goes deeply into the heart of every matter and extends far beyond the physical world of matter. Spirituality connects you with the profoundly powerful and divine force that's present in this universe. Whether you're looking for worldly success, inner peace, or supreme enlightenment, no knowledge can propel you to achieve your goals and provide as effective of a plan for living as does spiritual knowledge.

In life there are two approaches to living. There is a materialistic approach that relies primarily on the five senses to experience life. The materialistic approach is common for individuals who need evidence to prove its theories and day-to-day happening. What can be seen, heard, tasted, touched, and smelled is the basis for experiencing life. On the contrary there is a spiritual approach. This approach sees beyond the physical existence. Spirituality is extremely important in changing your language because this approach evokes change and uplifts the world by first transforming and improving his or her own vision or language.

One of the main teachings of spirituality is to look within and find what you seek within yourself. The external world is short-lived, temporary, and ever changing. In fact, your body will die one day sweeping all those worldly accoutrements away like a mere pile of dust. Your inner realm, on the other hand, is timeless, eternal, and deeply proud.

Embracing the reality that we are spiritual beings having a natural experience is the key tenant that helped me heal from my parent's death. I began to understand that connecting spiritually is what is most important. There is far more than the physical world and we all desire to experience that place.

Do you feel you are spiritually connected? Do I have a quiet center to my life? Is my life improving as a cause of my spirituality? Can you separate spirituality from personality?

_____

_____

_____

_____

CHAPTER 4

SPIRITUALITY VERSUS RELIGION

Although religion and spirituality are sometimes used interchangeably, they really indicate two different aspects of the human experience. You might say that spirituality is the mystical face of religion. I grew up in a very religious home. My father was a Baptist minister. We were at church every time the doors opened. My parents taught us to pray daily and we even had to memorize scriptures. While attending church we yielded to some strict religious practices. I am not certain I was taught the true meaning of spirituality, instead the Baptist religion is what was instilled in me. While I do feel religiosity has its value and place, in my opinion it should be coupled with a deep understanding of spirituality.

Spirituality is the wellspring of divinity that pulsates, dances, and flows as the source and essence of every soul. Spirituality relates more to your personal search, to finding greater meaning and purpose in your existence. Much like I had to find a greater meaning and purpose for my life after the death of both my parents. This encompassed me tapping into who I was at the core. Identifying who you are at the very core is a key component in changing your personal confessions. We live in a world where there are constant figures that contradict who we believe we are. Images in the media consistently tell us we are one thing and there is a constant battle with who we really are. Defining your life's purpose and pursuing that requires first knowing who you were placed here to be. Then and only then can you begin to speak positively over yourself, your environment, and all that is connected to you. Some elements of spirituality include the following:

- Looking beyond outer appearances to the deeper significance and soul of everything

- Love and respect for God

- Love and respect for yourself

- Love and respect for all others

Religion is most often used to describe an organized group or culture that has generally been sparked by the fire of a spiritual or divine soul. Religions usually act with a mission and intention of presenting specific teachings and doctrines while nurturing and propagating a particular way of life. Spirituality is a state of consciousness –it can exist with or without a religious belief.

Religion and Spirituality: A Beautiful Blend

Different religions can look quite unlike one another. Some participants bow to colorful statues of deities, others listen to inspired sermons while dressed in their Sunday finery, and yet others set out their prayer rugs five times a day to bow their heads to the ground. Regardless of these different outer manifestations of worship, the kernel of religion is spirituality, and the essence of spirituality is God.

Spirituality is:

- Beyond all religions yet containing all religions

- Beyond all science yet containing all science

- Beyond all philosophy yet containing all philosophy

As one becomes more spiritual, animalistic aggressions of fighting and trying to control the beliefs of other people can be cast off like an old set of clothes that no longer fit. In fact, many seekers begin to feel that every image of divinity is just one more face of their own, eternally ever-present God.

Loving and respecting all religions and images of God doesn't mean that you have to agree with all their doctrines. In fact, you don't even have to believe and agree with every element and doctrine of your own religion! This goes for any teachings you may encounter along your path. Everybody thinks that what they believe and how they worship is right. That's what's so funny about the world. Everybody is doing something different, and each one believes deep in his soul that his religion is the supreme way — some with more contemplation and conviction than others.

My personal journey of self-acceptance, faith, and freedom... while it is so scary and ambiguous, the more I travel this road the more comfortable and confident I become with simply allowing the journey to just be. Spirituality is relinquishing the desire to control everything, to embrace the unknown, and trusting that the universe will respond with great reciprocity of what's been given. I am a spiritual being with all divinity inside of me! In *Man's Search for Meaning* by Viktor Frankl, he suggests that happiness cannot be pursued, it must ensue. It awakens, arises, and appears. Happiness is a superpower.

Ask yourself: What function does spirituality serve in my life? Am I a whole person without my spirituality? Is spirituality tied to any emotions? Am I becoming more spiritual throughout my life?

CHAPTER 5

BECOMING YOUR HIGHER SELF

Joel Osteen, an American preacher, televangelist, author, and the Senior Pastor of Lakewood Church says, "Change the way you speak about yourself and you can change your life."

Speak affirmatively about yourself. When you begin to practice this you will be amazed to discover the increased strength you gain emotionally, spiritually, and most importantly, you are shaping the image on the inside to become your higher self. Rising higher is all up to you.

An ancient proverb says, "Whatever you send out comes back to you." As you go throughout your day – as you are driving, as you are dressing the children, as you are taking a shower, working at your desk or even cooking dinner – in a small voice, declare positive spiritually accurate statements about yourself. Abundance is my birthright. I am an overcomer. My steps are ordered. Therefore, I have Infinite Power divinely at work inside of me. I can accomplish all that I set out to do easily and effectively. The Scripture tells us to "call those things that are not as though they already are." In other words, don't spend time talking about what you are not. Instead, talk about what you desire to be. After all, this is the very essence of who we are. We are faith beings; Spirit begins ready to rise to our higher self.

Spirituality is vital because it actually pivots how we view life. In the physical realm, you have to see it to believe it. Spiritually God says, you have to believe it then you will see it. For example, I was an extreme procrastinator and undisciplined. I often talked about my lack of discipline. It wasn't until I started to reframe my language and speak affirmatively about being disciplined that it manifested in my life. It takes courage to rise to your higher self. You must have the courage to accurately call in what you need and desire.

Perhaps God has whispered something to your heart that seems humanly impossible. It may seem impossible for you to find the true love that you have always desired. It may seem impossible to launch that big business you've envisioned. It may seem impossible for you to gain that degree that you've always sought after. If you are anything like me, the odds are not in your favor in the physical realm. The odds are stacked against you and you don't see how it could happen for you. The great news is this is all a misconception when viewed in the spiritual realm. If you are truly ready to see those dreams manifest you must get your mouth moving in the right direction. Use your words to help you develop a new image on the inside. No matter how impossible something looks, start declaring boldly, "My dream is possible. My business is possible. My peace and infinite love is possible. I am Possible. Today I choose to rise higher."

Ask yourself: What things do I do that help me feel spiritual? Do I balance my spiritual needs with my daily schedule? Why or why not? What things help me feel spiritually healthy?

_____

_____

_____

_____

_____

_____

_____

CHAPTER 6

REDEFINE THE LINES AND SPACES IN YOUR LIFE

I was inspired while reading Man's Search for Meaning by Viktor Frankl. "Between stimulus and response, there is a space. In that space is our power to choose our response. In our response lie our growth and our freedom." ~ Viktor Frankl

I immediately felt the need to start writing about what happens "between the lines and spaces" of life.

There's always something in between the lines and spaces of life. There is a series of moments where you are figuring things out. The lines are definite and clear. There is nothing uncertain when it's on a line. It's time to win or lose, forgive or remain angry, be sharp or be flat. We are all familiar with the lines. Usually our comfort zones lie in state here. I like to call the lines, the "safe places."

In the spaces, we are open to life and open to listen. Here we see with our eyes wide open. We move with our whole heart and nothing else. We are completely uninhibited and free. Ready to experience what life has to offer. Daily we embrace the thought that nothing is for certain, but everything is possible. Yet we are gripped by fear.

So often we harness ourselves in ways that really don't serve us. We get overly concerned about what other people will think, and in the process we lose opportunities to express ourselves and be a little freer, a little more creative, a little more uniquely ourselves.

It starts early. We want to fit in, so we learn how to dress like others, move like others, eat like others, and speak like others whom we know. On one level, this isn't a bad thing. We do need to learn how to be social in ways that create harmonious environments. However, when we limit our creative potential, freedom and our authenticity, it is unhealthy and arresting.

Take dancing for example. Dancing is a great way to cut loose and release some pinned up energy, get a bit creative, and experience the freedom that movement brings. I'm always interested in how people respond to the activity of dance. Some people are totally free when they move, and others are rigid and tend to limit themselves. I can see how hard it is for them to just move and let their body talk without their mind completely dominating the conversation.

We are so acculturated to worry about "how we look" we often totally forget how to move just for the sake of "how it feels."

Awhile back, I was listening to an online radio show that is well known for encouraging others as it pertained to living freely and embracing their higher self. The host told this hilarious story about how she was at the airport when her flight was delayed by two hours. Did she get a cup of coffee and read the paper? Did she zone out in front of the TV?

No. She BUILT A FORT with a chair, her luggage carrier and a cape and then crawled into it. This is a grown woman I'm talking about here. Now, I'm not saying everyone should build forts in the airport. That may not be your thing. However, I am saying, wouldn't it be great if each of us could free up the need to fit in just long enough to have some fun, draw outside the lines and be creative, even if it wasn't what everyone else is doing? What if we could love ourselves enough to be authentically who we are in ways that set us free, and give permission for others to be free as well?

Loosen up. Draw outside the lines. Be free and above all, BE YOURSELF. Everyone else is taken. I vow to go freely through the minutes of life between the lines and spaces.

AFFIRMATION FOR MY TRUTH IS AT THE CORE OF MY BEING

I am calm and conscious. I intuitively know the right thing
to do moment to moment.
My inner compass is there to guide me when I need clarity, inner peace, wisdom,
creativity, inspiration, love, and companionship.
The world is a better place because of what I create.
Abundance is my birthright and I have access to everything in the universe.
My smallest action makes a difference. My life is important. I am changing the
world by just being here.
I am the person I was meant to become.
My personal truth and identity is how God views me.
Manifest It

Ask yourself – What would you do differently if you knew no one would judge you? Are you holding on to something you need to let go of?

_____

_____

_____

_____

_____

_____

_____

_____

_____

_____

CHAPTER 7

HOW FOCUS CAN CHANGE YOUR LIFE

One of the secrets of being happy, fulfilled and having a developed life is expressed in the words, "your focus is your reality." Look deeply into the meaning of this phrase. Can it be true that what you spend your time thinking about can actually manifest itself, in one way or another, in your life? The unequivocal answer is yes; your thoughts will guide you to your reality. Where your attention goes, your energy flows.

Take into account the vast thoughts that pass through your mind each day. If you are basically a happy person, you think optimistically. On the contrary, if you are constantly concerned with negativity, such as worrying about how you will get by with enough money to make it through the month, then those exact thoughts will determine how you feel. Those very thoughts will become your reality. The great part is that the choice is yours. You can grow, develop, and enjoy abundance or you can allow negative thoughts to rule your life.

Now focus your mind on positive things, if possible, meditate on them in relation to where you feel you are now. If you are not happy with what you see; CHANGE WHAT YOU SAY. Change your thoughts in a way that reflects how you would like things to be. From the moment you begin choosing only thoughts that will take you where you want to be, they will start to become your reality.

AFFIRMATIONS FOR YOUR FOCUS IS YOUR REALITY

My focus is my reality.
My mind is precise and clear as I apply it to any situation.
I can focus on anything and get positive results.
I choose my reality and how I want my life to be.
I take time to relax and unwind.
I can achieve whatever I want if I take time to focus on a positive outcome.
I sleep well as my systems recharge and give me plenty of energy.
My brain operates in an efficient and balanced manner.
I only have to ask my Creator for answers and I will receive them quickly and
always for my best interest.
I eat a healthy diet and I exercise whenever possible, this keeps my brain
in optimal condition.

Ask yourself, if you had a friend that spoke to you the same way you speak to yourself, would you still be their friend? If you were to die tomorrow, what would you regret not doing, being, saying, or having in your life?

_____

_____

_____

_____

_____

_____

_____

_____

_____

CHAPTER 8

ADJECTIVES THAT RULE OUR WORLD

Have you heard – pick your poison? Well words can be poison to our souls and livelihood, especially when we do not choose well. However, depending on what you take from a word will also affect how it affects your life. If you choose to just focus on the negativity, you will receive negativity back from the universe. Follow along as I show how certain words can mean doom but can be looked at in a manner that can bring enlightenment.

Adversity or Achievement

Adversity – a condition marked by misfortune; a state, condition, or instance of serious hardship

Achievement – a thing done successfully, typically by effort, courage, or skill.

Either you can chose to magnify the adversity you face or to celebrate the achievements you make. In life we will experience hardship/adversity. It seems that each issue you face is magnified times two because you seemingly face it alone. However, adversity can lead to victory/achievement. Yes, it's another battle but one you never have to fight alone. It is great to know that God never intends for you to endure life alone. In His word He tells you He will never leave you nor forsake you (Deuteronomy 31:6). God promises you His presence. Embrace your number one support system. God!

Achievement Prayer

Lord, I pray that I am able to celebrate each achievement, no matter how small. Help me to lessen the attention given to adversity and increase the attention given to triumph. In Jesus' name, Amen.

1. What adversities have you faced?

_____

_____

_____

2. How can those adversities be turned into achievements?

_____

_____

_____

List 3 Achievements.

1. _____

_____

_____

2. _____

_____

_____

3. _____

_____

_____

Broken or Bold

Broken – the characteristic of no longer being whole or in working order; God's requirement for maximum usefulness

Bold – willing to face anything with courage/bravery; showing confidence; not being afraid of difficult situations

Coming to grips with your brokenness is not the easiest. Often times, this reality causes feelings of unresolved hurt that are deeply buried. In this world, broken things are despised and thrown out. Anything we no longer need, we throw away. Damaged goods are rejected, and that includes people. The world is full of people with broken hearts, broken spirits, and broken relationships. The beauty in this brokenness is your ability to glean boldly like the work of art you are. Yes, you! You are a mosaic with tiny pieces carefully put together by a fine craftsman. By all means, don't waddle in your brokenness. You were broken for a specific purpose. The Lord is close to the broken-hearted and saves those who are crushed in spirit (Psalm 34:18). There is something about a broken point that causes you to seek the Lord more sincerely. Think about it. God can take what has been broken and make it into something better. After all, Jesus' body was broken for us. And because of this brokenness we can declare BOLDLY and FEARLESSLY that we are whole.

Boldness Prayer

Lord, cause me to see that I was broken for a purpose. Open my heart to understand that through you I am whole. Give me the boldness to fearlessly declare that you are the restorer of my soul. Cause me to love myself and my life with the Love of Christ.

I BOLDLY declare that today I am made whole through Christ and that I am...

_____

_____

_____

Catastrophic or Contentment

Catastrophic - causing great and often sudden distress, life threatening

Contentment – a state of happiness and satisfaction

Contentment is not the fulfillment of what you want; instead it is the realization of what you already have. Contentment is feeling fine with what you have and who you are in this moment. It is easy to get caught up in great distress fixating on what you don't have and what you need or want. The challenge for you today is to shift your focus from misfortune to gratification. Although catastrophes may exist on the exterior, the beauty of contentment is an internal satisfaction that is not predicated on external circumstances. I know what it is to be in need, and I know what it is to have plenty. I have learned the secret of being content in any and every situation, whether well fed or hungry, whether living in plenty or in want (Philippians 4:12).

Contentment Prayer

Lord, teach me to be content in my current state. Cause me to experience sincere internal happiness despite what it looks like today. In Jesus name, Amen.

Today I am content with my current...

1. _____
   _____
   _____
   _____
   _____
   _____

2. _____
   _____
   _____
   _____
   _____
   _____

3. _____
   _____
   _____
   _____
   _____
   _____

CHAPTER 9

LIFE-ENRICHING LANGUAGE PRACTICE POINTS

1. Language starts with thought. Pay attention to your thoughts, and whenever you catch yourself in a negative thought pattern, bring it to a screeching halt. Immediately say out loud, "Stop!" Break the pattern by speaking or singing something to distract you from the negative thoughts. Repeat this for five minutes to unlock the negative pattern.

2. Start your day with verbal intention. When you wake up, go to your mirror and have a chat with yourself. State out loud your intention for how your day will proceed. For example, say something like, "I intend to have a joyful, fun and productive day filled with positive and successful interactions and events."

3. Use car time as self-talk time. As an international speaker, I use time in the car to practice my speaking skills out loud. Instead of listening to negative news on the radio or feeling anxious about traffic, use the time in the car to repeat positive affirmations about yourself or to rehearse a positive conversation or presentation. You may feel goofy doing this, but do it anyway. This verbal activity will reinforce the feelings behind the words you are speaking.

4. Disengage from negative conversations. When other people start venting about their day or some co-worker or politics, politely excuse yourself from the conversation. If that's not possible, do what you can to steer the conversation in a more positive direction. Whatever you do, don't participate in this pessimistic discourse. There is nothing positive that will come from it.

5. Express gratitude. Several times a day, take a moment to look around you and verbally acknowledge what you are grateful for. I just did this little exercise as I am writing and expressed gratitude for my computer, my ability to write, and the people who will be reading my book, the bird on the limb outside my window, the books on my desk. You get the picture. Good things are all around us, and if we take the time to see them and speak thanks for them, we begin to feel uplifted and happy.

6. Follow difficult words with action words. There are times when we do have to speak about negative, painful or unpleasant things. During these times, speaking about our pain helps us unburden ourselves from it. It is a necessary part of healing. But once the burden begins to lift, follow up with words and discussion around healing and action. Speak about feeling better and moving forward even before you feel ready to do so. You will be paving the path for yourself as you take the first step toward healing and happiness.

7. Include writing in the mix. If you really want to give your brain a double whammy, write down your affirmations, words of gratitude or positive thoughts, before you speak them. Writing about these ideas is another reinforcing action step that sends signals to the pre-frontal cortex, stimulating feelings of joy.

8. Do the work consistently. Strengthening your brain and transforming your thoughts and feelings takes practice. Like exercise, the work must be done regularly and with intensity if you want to see results.

Commit to pro-actively speaking positive affirmations and words of gratitude at least three times a day. Pay attention to your thoughts and words all the time. Regularly remove yourself from negative conversations. Rate your level of happiness and contentment on a scale of one to ten as you begin this work, and then rate yourself again after a month or two to see how you are progressing.

Positive, powerful words are tools that can set you free and change your life. Choose them wisely.

_____

_____

_____

_____

_____

_____

_____

_____

_____

_____

_____

_____

_____

_____

_____

_____

_____

_____

_____

_____

_____

_____

_____

_____

_____

CHAPTER 10

HOW POSITIVE SPEAKING CAN IMPACT YOUR LIFE

A Pep Talk in Every Breath

The power of speaking positively is like a car with a powerful engine that can take you to the summit of a mountain. Positive speaking does not mean you keep your head in the sand and ignore life's unpleasant realities. On the contrary, it means that you will approach life's roller coasters with a positive mind and an optimistic outlook. I will never forget being in high school and attending one pep rally after another every stinking week. I often wondered why we had pep rallies if our football team kept losing. My thoughts, "what's the sense in celebrating a losing team?' Then years later when I had to be my own personal cheerleader after failing in life over and over again, is when I fully understood the necessity of the "pep rally". It does not matter what life throws your way, make the decision to look at yourself in the mirror and give yourself the best pep talk ever. It is perfectly fine to pour words of affirmation back into yourself.

Psychologists define self-talk as intrapersonal communication or communication occurring in the mind of the individual in a model which contains a send/receive, and feedback loop. In short, we are wired so uniquely that we have the power to control the internal communications so much so that our entire life can be changed simply by how we think and speak. My encouragements to you today are go to the mirror, look at yourself, and create the best personal pep talk every day. You must talk like you are in the fourth quarter of the game and the time clock is running down, you are tired of losing, and everything you have is depending on this one last play.

Tell yourself, I WILL WIN!

Don't get me wrong – we all have our weak moments. Example: I woke up this morning feeling a bit lethargic with the urge to stretch wide and long. As I stretched, I said out loud, "I'm READY" while thinking about my long to-do list questioning if I really believed those words. As I walked about the house a bit more, stretched some more, contemplated some more I continued to tell myself – "I AM READY! I GOT THIS!" Once I was at work I was ready to take on the day and took control over how my day would play out simply by using positive self-talk. For me, words are a form of action, capable of influencing change. In my best James Brown voice I am singing, "I feel good!" It is your privilege to tell your day exactly what you expect from it. Don't forget! What we say to ourselves hues our thinking which in turn paints what our lives reflect!

When you find yourself not being your best personal cheerleader, ask yourself - What is my evidence for and against my thinking? Am I jumping to negative conclusions? How can I find out if my thoughts are actually true? If I were being positive, how would I perceive this situation? And the big one – will this situation really matter in five years?

CHAPTER 11

START SAYING "I CAN!" INVITE FAITH NOT FEAR

When you say "I can't", and expect the worst, you become weak and unhappy. When you say "I can", and expect success, you fill yourself with confidence and happiness. If you think you can, YOU CAN. If you think you can't, YOU CAN'T. Fear comes in the thinking, confidence comes in the doing. By all means, take the time to think it through and think it over and when that ends it is time to start acting. I will never forget when God showed me He wanted me to serve in Africa. I was scared out of my mind. I have always watched the news and of course those things I saw previously began to creep up in my mind. My thoughts went from how will I finance this trip to what if there is a war and I am killed? In my mind, I had already aborted the mission based on fear of the unknown.

The National Institute of Mental Health suggests that 90% of the things we fear will never take place. I found this to be very true after experiencing one of the most life changing moments ever in East Africa. I kept asking myself, *what would life be like if I allowed myself to remain arrested by fear?* After finally facing my fear and accomplishing the intended goal of traveling to Africa, I vowed to always face my fear head on. Sometimes confronting fears head-on is the best way to overcome them.

Here are a few easy ways to harness fear and activate faith. First you must analyze your fear. By owning the source of your fear you've taken the first step towards gaining control over the situation. Write it down. Writing is communicating. Let your fear rise to the surface and give it a name. Once you've named it you are then able to speak directly to the source. Secondly, imagine the outcome of the desire. After all, the desired outcome has a much greater reward than the fear. Do yourself a favor, paint the most elaborate story in your head of what you desire to accomplish. Keep your pen and paper handy to list all the rewards, gratifications and satisfactions that are waiting for you beyond the fear. Creating this story is only the beginning of activating your faith. Lastly, change the way you think about fear. Reframe your fear in a positive light. See fear as an opportunity. Once the discomfort of the initial wave of fear passes, rewrite the embellished story that resided in your head, and you'll see all of the opportunities that are on the other side of fear…At that point, you will be well on your way to living a fulfilled and fearless, enriched life of faith. Your mantra will then become, "I will use Fear as Fuel to take my life to the next level."

Think of all the things that are keeping you from moving on to the next step in your life goals. Now ask yourself - What self-thoughts are sabotaging your progress? Are these thoughts rational, and based on any clear facts? Are past unsuccessful attempts unnecessarily preventing you from making a positive change?

CHAPTER 12

WHEN LIFE GETS TIGHT, GET TOUGH AND SPEAK UP

It is in tight places that we scream the loudest. I will never forget as a child the day I smashed my finger in the door. I yelled, "OUCH" because it hurt so badly. I could not stop yelling because of the pain I was enduring. Today, I am reminded of that moment as I think on some personal "door slamming" situations in my adult life. I am sure you can identify with the moment when life literally squeezed you to your limits. We have all had those internal screams that no one else can hear. It is those moments that we must realize how essential it is to speak the right words to gain release and relief. When life gets tight and tough…SPEAK UP! What does that look like? Here it is. Think about the positive things that are going on in your life. Create a personal mantra; be sure to use some of your most positive experiences. Repeat this mantra both morning and night. Focusing on these positives will keep negative thoughts from finding their way into your mind and therefore reducing the frequency of stressful emotions.

Studies suggest that optimism and pessimism may affect your quality of life. Optimistic communication enables you to cope better with stressful situations. When life begins to squeeze the blood out of you, think about your anxiety as a reaction to the event rather than the event itself. Exploring your spirituality can lead to a clearer mental pathway and a better view of your life's purpose. Meditation is a form of spiritual communication. In my personal most stressful moments I have found my inner peace and calmness through meditation. In the beginning, when I first started utilizing the power of meditation I found it difficult if not almost impossible for me to focus. I even questioned its purpose. My thoughts were if you have any bit of a life, it can be difficult to take 10 to 15 minutes out of your day to simply shut your brain down. I couldn't even do that while I slept back then and thought 'how in the world will I be able to accomplish this while wide awake?' I can't believe for a minute I was the only one like this as a beginner. But still the same, I am hard headed and refuse to just give up on something without giving it a diligent effort. I would have to say after about a week of allowing myself to be thought free for those 15 minutes or so daily I began to look forward to them. However I had to give myself permission to let go of the control for those 15 minutes. To allow deadlines to be put on the back-burner and everything else that would muddle my mind. In giving myself that permission I gave myself peace – pure peaceful unadulterated PEACE. I gained a whole new insight to just how powerful I could be if I just learned to give myself permission to be in touch with myself.

When was the last time you spoke up to yourself? When have you ever told yourself that you were going to do something no matter what else was lurking in the background?

_____

_____

_____

_____

_____

_____

_____

_____

_____

_____

CHAPTER 13

LET THE WORLD BE SEEN THROUGH YOUR EYES

The difference between can and cannot is only three letters. These three letters can change the direction of your life. Positive and negative are directions. Which direction will you choose?

Positive thinking is expecting, talking, believing, and visualizing what you want, as an accomplished fact. Riches, mediocrity, and poverty begin in the mind. Reality is the mirror of your thoughts. Choose well, what you put in front of the mirror. A positive attitude awakens inner strength, energy, motivation, and initiative. Reading and reciting a few positive thoughts before bed and in the morning, will change your mindset, transform your life and attract good things to you.

Affirm the positive, visualize the positive and expect the positive and your life will change accordingly. When there are difficulties and you are down… Visualize, Think and Expect the positive. Don't let circumstances influence your thoughts and moods. Choose your thoughts and soon your life will mirror those thoughts. Fill your mind with light, happiness, hope, feelings of security, and strength and soon your life will reflect these qualities.

Coping skills are important as they keep us cool, calm, and collected. During those days that are unbelievably trying, repeat inspiring quotes throughout your day. This will help you to gain a better perspective on things and cope with circumstances that arise.

If you have yet to hone in on your own personal coping skills, here are a few other suggestions that will help you get better control when all seems totally out of control:

Self-talk - Focus on the positives about yourself and or the situation rather than the negatives. I was told once that there are 10 positives to every negative if you think on it hard enough. Dig deep and find the positives.

Support Group – I am not talking about necessarily a group that meets weekly at a local church; just people you know who are in your corner who will help you see the positives. Not those people who will wallow with you or begin wallowing on their own situations. We all know someone like that. Steer clear. You want a person who is willing to give you a different perspective on the situation.

Relax – YES! Relax! Why is it that we find that the hardest thing to give ourselves permission to do yet it is one of the most essential things we must do! Just breathe. That little downtime can create miracles!

Distraction can be your friend – Change your focus for a while. Find something else to put your energies into and you will be surprised when you come back to revisit the problem you have a different outlook or outcome. Have you ever lost something in your home and you frantically go about trying to locate it? In your frantic state you never do find it but as soon as you place your focus elsewhere it seems to magically appear.

When you're faced with a difficult situation, an important question to ask is:

What's the best thing I can do to resolve this problem? Write down all the alternatives you can think of then break them each down from there to find the solution that will work best for you.

Famous Artist Vincent Van Gogh once stated, "If you hear a voice within saying, 'You are not a painter' then by all means paint and that voice will be silenced." The greatest technique to silencing your internal naysayer is conscious life-enriching self-talk followed by intentional actions. Today I encourage you to silence that internal naysayer, commit to positive self-talk, and allow your life to flow from the inside out!

Take the time and space now to write down anything that you are struggling with. Look at those items and try to come up with 3 solutions to each. If you begin to feel stress during this exercise, practice your coping skills – revisit it and see what new you can add to your solutions.

_____

_____

_____

_____

_____

_____

_____

_____

_____

_____

_____

_____

_____

_____

_____

_____

_____

_____

_____

_____

_____

_____

_____

_____

_____

_____

_____

_____

_____

_____

_____

_____

_____

_____

_____

_____

_____

_____

_____

_____

_____

_____

_____

_____

CHAPTER 14

ARE YOU PRESENT?

The time is now. Stay in the present. You can't do anything to change the past and the future will come. How it comes will be determined on if you are staying present or living in the past; if you are actively planning your future for success or sabotaging it by reflecting on yesteryears.

Start today not tomorrow; if anything you should have started yesterday.

Many of you, myself included, have laid out the plan for the year. As you move forward be sure to hold that vision, business plan, vision board, big idea, and/or dream before The Lord. Don't move with such haste to accomplish the goal that you miss the journey. Allow the Vision Giver to set the pace and enjoy it as it unfolds moment by moment! I promise that his perfect timing will always trump your strategic timeline of target dates. By all means, have a plan but don't forget to consult the Plan Giver!

As you think about your goals be sure they are...

1. Clear enough to be kept in focus?

2. Close enough to be achieved?

3. Helpful enough to change lives?

Ask yourself these questions...

1. Is what I am doing now getting me closer to my goals?

2. Am I headed in a direction that helps me to fulfill my commitments, maintain my priorities, and realize my dreams?

In addition, within the next 24 hours make an appointment with yourself to WRITE YOUR PLANS DOWN! Yes, jot down on the calendar – "Appointment with VIP – Me!"

I have noticed lately I think more intensely than ever about my future. I guess that's what happens when you age. My thoughts have been vast covering thoughts of my family to my faith and even my finances. However the main questions that kept dauntingly reappearing in my thoughts were "What is success?" "How do I define success?" And the most frightening of all of them, "AM I SUCCESSFUL?" I'll be honest. It took some true reflection, soul searching, defining, and redefining for me to come up with an unequivocal...YES, I AM SUCCESSFUL!

At one time, I viewed success as a destination or place where I would arrive. I defined it as the advanced recognition of a predetermined, yet worthwhile goal. Excitedly, I can say over time and with experiencing life that I have realized my definition does not ring true and falls short of the mark of what true success is. NEWSFLASH: The "I made it, I am a success" scheme is how unsuccessful people see success: as something to strive for or hope to reach "someday." My encouragement to you today is, do not use other's achievements as a barometer to measure your success. Take a few moments to mentally recollect all your accomplishment, hardships, flaws, triumphs, and even shortcomings. Find the nearest mirror; take a good look and say, "THIS IS WHAT SUCCESS LOOKS LIKE!" You were created by the master of success and in his image – therefore you are success!

Use this space to write down all the things you have been successful at. Yes, Brag about YOU!!

_____

_____

_____

_____

_____

_____

_____

_____

_____

_____

_____

_____

_____

_____

_____

_____

_____

_____

_____

_____

_____

_____

_____

_____

_____

_____

_____

_____

_____

CHAPTER 15

MARCH FORWARD

"General, your tank is a powerful vehicle. It smashes down forests and crushes a hundred men. But it has one defect: it needs a driver." ~ Bertolt Brecht

Time waits for no one. The battle has begun. You are a part of the war whether you like it or not. While this sounds brash and a bit harsh to say, this is the reality for every person existing. The best part of it all is you have a choice. You can either refuse to fight and die or march forward with the power that's inside of you.

Take a moment and look at where you are today compared to where you were 1 year ago, 5 years ago, and even 10 years ago. Celebrate the gains you have made over time – each gain is a success in its own. It doesn't all have to be finances and fancy cars or even a wedding ring on your finger. It could be that you have chosen to take better care of yourself, you managed to keep the laundry under control for a year or you are celebrating 10 years in your employment. No matter how big or small, you need to celebrate that success. The world is full of demands from you. If you don't create some demands for yourself the world will eat you up with theirs. Start with demanding that you acknowledge what you have accomplished versus what you have yet to do.

What does it mean to make demands for your life? What would that look like every day if you were your own personal drill sergeant? Answer these questions in the space provided below. In reflecting on them, how many of the answer can you generate into life goals?

I demand the right to –

_____

_____

_____

_____

I demand an immediate end to –

_____

_____

_____

_____

I demand adequate –

_____

_____

_____

_____

I demand that all those involved will –

_____

_____

_____

_____

_____

CHAPTER 16

SEE CHANGE AND BE CHANGE

"We need to be the change we wish to see in the world." ~Mahatma Ghandi

Positive thoughts are not enough. There has to be positive feelings and positive actions. When you have control over your thoughts you have control over your life. By using positive words you send out positive high-energy vibrations. As we know from the Law of Attraction, similar vibrations will be attracted back to you. Before you speak, think about what your words will attract. If you're like most people, you only want the best coming back to you. Let your words emphasize those actions.

Continue using positive words for every situation in your life. It takes some practice but it can actually be a lot of fun. Treat it like a game and learn a new positive word or phrase every day. Then go out and share those words with others. Before you know it, you will have created an entirely new and uplifting language!

This essentially is how the world is transformed completely. I can remember times in my life when I would say things like, "This job is killing me." Whoa! Those words are powerful. While my job wasn't killing me physically it was killing me financially and mentally too. I would wake up in the morning and dread getting up. I despised the sound of my alarm clock. I got to the point I didn't even have enough energy left in me to care about other things in my life that were important to me because my job was sucking the life right out of me. Truth be told, although my job was demanding, I was the one sucking the life right out of me. I was the one feeding the dragon foray by how I used my free time and by what I spoke into my work environment mind. Was I using my off hours to speak energy and goodwill into my life? No, I spent the majority of that time complaining about how tired I was from work, stressed, and how I felt underappreciated. What I should have been doing was speaking life into my free time; thanking God I had a job, roof over my head and food on my table. This would have given me a new found energy every time I faced a work day. In addition, rather than speaking gloom and doom into my work days I should have been giving thanks for having a place to make an income and looked for all the other positives that came with my employment. It wasn't until I changed my mindset that work no longer felt as dreaded but not only that, I had a new found confidence in myself and the ambition again to move on to the next journey in my life.

If you sit back and do nothing but complain, nothing is going to change. It isn't until you start taking the necessary steps to improve not only your attitude but overall life that you will begin to see the change you want to be and have others see.

What can you say to yourself that is positive or encouraging?

CHAPTER 17

GIVE UP OR GO ON

So many times it just seems easier to toss in the towel and call it quits than it is to fix or trudge through to get to the other side of a situation. Deciding when to give up or continue on isn't always an easy answer to come up with. However we are in a society that is in love with instant gratification so many give up far before they even try to complete something because the reward isn't coming fast enough. Example: The Internet, although a plethora of information, doesn't have absolutely everything. A friend of mine was working on a college term paper assignment and was utilizing the Internet to locate various studies done on her topic. When she couldn't find what she was looking for she decided to use one of her life lines – choices being 1. Call a friend – and 2. Hit the local library. She chose the first and called me asking various questions as if I was to be an expert in that particular field with the ability to drop stats as such. Sadly to say, she blew that lifeline and eventually blew her paper. Rather than taking my suggestion of hitting the local library that was full of the knowledge she was looking for she basically just gave up and in return handed in a less than satisfactory paper.

Nothing in life comes easy, but everything can come as long as you don't give up. The saying – Rome wasn't built in a day is a perfect example. Think what the world would be like if full of quitters. What would we have? Would you even be here yourself?

Going on takes determination, courage, and faith. Faith that once you obtain your desired destination that God will be there yet we forget by going on God is driving the show the entire way. You are never alone in your journeys.

Think of times that you have wanted to give up and didn't. That you powered through. How did that make you feel when you got to the other side? Now think of times that you had given up. How did that make you feel? Is there anything you think you could have done differently to get to the other side of the situation rather than giving up now as you look back? Did you really give up or did you go on?

_____

_____

_____

_____

_____

_____

_____

_____

_____

_____

_____

_____

_____

_____

_____

_____

_____

_____

CHAPTER 18

LET THE LIGHT SHINE IN

In life, there are so many things that can darken our moments, from death to troubled relationships, job loss, rejection, and so much more. When faced with troubling times it is understandable that you would want to lock yourself in your room and not come out ever! It is human nature and almost like a protection mode – hide so no more pain can find its way in. Yet, when we hide, if for too long, we don't let the light in either. We block ourselves from our blessings – things that God has meant for us alone.

In life we are given free choice. There is no one – and I mean no one that can stop you from doing or not doing anything. People can tell you no – threaten you, even leave you when they don't like a direction you choose to go, but no one can actually stop you. Not even God will take free choice away from you. It is a gift he has given all and it is up to the receiver to use that gift wisely. Unfortunately, there will always be those that take that free will to make very bad choices, choices that even put others in jeopardy or worse. Think of a robber – they can make the choice to get a job and work for what they want or think they need or they can choose to rob another that has put the work in to obtain those items. With every choice there is a consequence. There are only two outcomes – good or bad.

You can choose to close the windows and darken your room, or you can open the windows and let the light in. It is a matter of choice. Your mind is your room. Do you darken it or let the light in? Train your mind to think in terms of "it is possible and it can be done." Use your mind and free will to let the light shine in and through you allow the light to be an infection that spreads on to others.

Think of your darkest moments in life. What did you do to come out of the dark into a better state? If you are facing a difficult time, think of ways that could allow some light to shine in. If you know of someone in a dark place; what can you do that could possibly bring some light into their life.

_____

_____

_____

_____

_____

_____

_____

_____

_____

_____

_____

_____

_____

_____

_____

_____

_____

_____

_____

_____

CHAPTER 19

I AM BECAUSE HE IS

We all have struggled at one point or another with the big question, "Who am I?" One thing I feel we all could agree on is we are all the child of our Heavenly Father, created in His image, and given the divine design to become God-like. We have been provided with unique gifts and talents to help us get to our true person. On the road to self-discovery of who we are gives our lives purpose and steers us to make the right choices in life. This doesn't mean it will always be an easy path – that there will be no bumps in the road – simply that we have been given the tools to discover who we are – it is up to us to utilize them for full discovery.

Who do you want to be? Better yet – who are you right now at this moment. Are you happy with that person? Are you comfortable in the skin you dwell in? What labels have been placed upon you by life or choice? If you do not like who you are at this moment in time or the labels that define you it is time you start challenging yourself to make the changes necessary to find who you were really meant to be.

You can begin by changing your thought pattern. The thoughts you have of yourself internalize and materialize who you become in your own mirror and in the eyes of others. This can be a positive or a negative image depending on the perspective of the viewer. Remember, if you think hard enough you can change a negative into a positive – drastic example – you have been labeled a drug addict – most would look at that as a negative right? What positive traits can you think of that a drug addict may possess? A few negative traits one would say are obsessive, controlling and devious. Okay – now how can we take those negative traits and turn them into positive self-talk? For one –

obsessive could be looked at as a strong desire to persevere. Controlling can be looked at as a strong desire to direct ones destiny, and devious could be looked at as a critical thinker. Although this is a drastic example, you can see how even negative traits or thoughts can be switched into something more desirable depending on one's perspective. Change your language and change your perspective on life. Even at your weakest you can expose your inner strengths. Transform your thought process and the rest will follow.

Stop comparing yourself to others. Define your values and be authentic to yourself. Remind yourself that you were created in greatness; you are exceptional and you are precious in God's eyes. Find your passion and make it your purpose in life. Like an artist, they have a vision in their mind of what their next masterpiece will be, however will never see the full picture until it is completed. Life is your palette and you are the paintbrush, the finished picture is who God has meant you to become. Start painting.

_____

_____

_____

_____

_____

_____

_____

_____

_____

_____

_____

_____

CHAPTER 20

STEP UP TO BE THE BEST YOU WERE MEANT TO BE

With the right attitude you can inspire yourself to be greater. Henry Ford said - "Don't find fault, find a remedy." It is so easy to come up with a million ways why something won't work rather than why it could work. The right attitude is not alone the great denominator to success or greatness. It is only one step on the ladder but a very important step to take as it is the foundation – your stability. Without it your ladder will crumble down to the fiery depths every time.

There is no one step to greatness and each person's greatness is unique to them. However by including all of the steps to climb to become the best you were meant to be, you can and will succeed.

When building your ladder to become the best you were meant to be there are several key steps you need on your ladder on top of a positive attitude. The additional steps needed are as follows:

Awareness - A strong awareness about the arena you see yourself in is essential. Without it you are just a viewer into another world and not an active participant. Get informed – read, listen, and surround yourself with others that have the knowledge you wish to obtain.

God Given Predisposition – Yes, God has already instilled in you your given talent. You are passionate about it and it is something you enjoy immensely. Have you tapped into that yet? You can easily tell what God has gifted you with by those things you can do easily with little to no effort.

They come to you as easily as breathing. That doesn't mean you can't hone that talent more, and often times that takes a lot of hard work, but it is work that will pay off in high dividends because you are following the gift that was God given.

Master Plan and Set Goals – You will never get to your destination with blinders on. You need to create a clear road map and set goals to obtain your final destination. Invest the time in creating that path. You are worth it.

FOCUS – Like with your master plan and goals, without a strong focus you will never accomplish what you set out to do. Make it a priority to work on your plan daily – it doesn't matter if it is only 15 minutes a day – no work towards your future leaves you empty handed.

Support – Rally your pep squad! Remember, winning or losing we all deserve a pep rally that is going to keep us amped or help rejuvenate our passion.

What positive attributes do you possess right now? What would you like to add to your arsenal?

_____

_____

_____

_____

_____

_____

_____

_____

_____

_____

CHAPTER 21

SMILE, EVEN WHEN YOU DON'T FEEL LIKE IT

Smiling is something that we do naturally, without much thought. We may see our children playing, or one of our friends do something silly, this will naturally cause us to smile. When we smile we are expressing our happiness, in that moment, with those around us. However, many of us tend to overlook the mind-body connection that takes place every time we smile. When we smile, we trigger our left frontal cortex, which just so happens to be the portion of our brain that is used to register happiness.

Since smiling triggers a mind-body connection, it is only natural that the more you smile the better you feel. Every time you smile, you send your brain a message that you are happy, and when you're happy your body produces endorphins that increase your good mood. So, if you find that you are not feeling as great as you would like, all you have to do is smile; even when you don't feel like it. As you begin to smile more, you will begin to notice that you are not as grumpy or drained at the end of the day.

Just as a simple smile can improve your overall level of happiness, it can also make those around you happy as well. Studies have shown that smiling is contagious. This means that when others are around your smiling face, they can't help but to begin smiling too. This is simply another reason why it is important that you find something to smile about each and every day. Whether it is seeing your best friend after a long time, or just remembering something funny that happened. Whatever makes you smile, make the time do more of it. Not only is it healthy for you, but it has a positive effect on those around you.

If you experience a high level of stress throughout the day, just smile. That simple act can help you reduce the symptoms associated with stress and anxiety. When you smile, you are signaling your brain that you're happy. Although you may not be feeling totally happy at the moment, the more you smile the happier you will become. As you relax, your body will slow your breathing and lower your heart rate; thereby reducing your levels of stress and anxiety.

Honestly, haven't you noticed that smiling just feels good? Smiling feels natural and improves your overall stress levels. When you smile more, you just begin to feel happy that you are alive and have the opportunity to share your life with those you love. So, the next time that you're in a bad mood, experiencing a high level of stress, or simply don't feel like smiling; smile, you'll be happy that you did.

Ask yourself - How Many Times Do You Smile Each Day? What is The Most Common Reason You Smile? Challenge yourself to make at least two other people smile a day.

_____

_____

_____

_____

_____

_____

_____

_____

_____

_____

CHAPTER 22

SET YOURSELF FREE!

Many people believe that they cannot enjoy their lives today because of something that has happened in their past. Perhaps they didn't do something in the way that was expected, or they lost something or someone who was extremely important to them, or they may have been deeply hurt which now affects the way that they give love and receive it. Whatever the case may be, these people are holding themselves prisoners because of their past.

What many of us fail to accept is that while we hold onto the past and the hurt and pain that it holds, we are only hurting ourselves. By refusing to live in the moment and enjoy the lives that we have, we are only hurting ourselves. What happened in the past is over and done with; we cannot change the outcome of any particular situation. In order to move forward in our lives, we have to accept what has happened and come to terms with it.

One of the first steps we can take to set ourselves free is to release the emotional attachment that we have to the past. If we can allow our memories to simply be memories, then they will have no control over our present lives. As we allow ourselves to release the pain and guilt associated with the memories that are holding us back, we can then simply allow them to become a memory and not a bar in the prison we have built for ourselves. This may be easier said than done, but if you are ready and willing to let go you can do it.

The next step in setting yourself free is to forgive. You will need to forgive yourself and others in order to successfully release yourself from your past. As you begin this process, you may come to realize that all of the times you have felt stuck in your life, you needed to forgive. When you forgive you will allow yourself to enjoy and live in the present without holding onto the pain of the past. When you hold onto fear, guilt, hurt, sadness, regret, and anger you are living in a state of un-forgiveness. When you allow yourself to forgive, you will allow love to flow freely.

Forgiveness can be one of the most difficult things you have to do. But for many of us it is a necessary step we must take before we can set ourselves free. We are not forgiving the person who caused us pain to absolve them of any guilt; we are forgiving them in order to allow ourselves to move forward. If we allow ourselves to remain stuck in the past or continue to relive a particular situation, we continue to give that person or situation control over our lives. Practice forgiveness and take the control back; once you do, you can begin to live in the present and enjoy the life you have created.

Ask yourself - What Is Holding You Back? What Will It Take For You To Let Go? Are You Ready To Take Control Of Your Past? Or Are You Resisting The Process?

_____

_____

_____

_____

_____

_____

_____

_____

_____

_____

_____

CHAPTER 23

LET'S HEAR YOUR BATTLE CRY

Successfully communicating your thoughts or feelings can be one of the most difficult tasks for a lot of people. Not only is it important to know what you're going to say and how you're going to say it; it is also important that you understand when the most appropriate time to say it is. It is common for people to sit back and not say anything when something should be said. Perhaps it is an observation, a suggestion, an idea, or even a criticism. For whatever reason, many people will choose to not speak up and allow the situation to pass.

It may be because they are afraid to hurt someone's feelings, or appearing to be mean. It can also be because they do not want to be embarrassed or cause any trouble. While it may seem like staying quiet is the best choice, it may not always be in your best interest. As uncomfortable as it may be, standing up and speaking your mind is the best choice you can make.

When you choose to remain silent, your silence may appear to be an approval of the situation. While remaining silent may keep you from becoming involved in the conflict that may be going on, it can actually be taken in the opposite note. In any type of situation where input is required, your refusal to speak up may end up causing you to be seen as part of the problem. It is common for people to recognize who said what and who spoke up during any type of conflict; this means that your refusal to speak up and voice your opinion may cause others to view your actions as a sign of approval. This can hurt you further down the road. It is rare that you will be appreciated for keeping your opinion to yourself. So, speak up and tell those around you how you feel and what your opinion is.

Speaking up is also a great way to demonstrate to others that you are invested in the situation. When you speak up you show that you are there because you care about the end result. You're not just taking up space, rather, you have an opinion as to what the best way to handle a situation may be. When you speak up, people view that as a form of honesty. Honesty goes a long way in the building of trust, especially when you can combine it with empathy. People will see that you are not afraid to be truthful, and that you care.

Your life experience and knowledge have value in a variety of situations. This can allow you to see things in a manner which others may not be able to. By refusing to speak up and share with others how you interpret a particular situation, that situation may become worse. If you can add a different perspective, you may be able to help resolve the situation in a shorter period of time. Never be afraid to use what life has taught you. If you refuse to share your opinion with others, you may regret it later on.

Ask yourself - How Can My Opinion Help? What Do I Have To Offer? Can I Help Improve The Situation By Speaking Up? What Keeps You From Speaking Up?

CHAPTER 24

POWER THROUGH

During the course of our lives we are faced with many different obstacles and challenges. We have the choice to either allow them to control us or power through to the other side. The decision lies within our choices and strength. If we choose to power through, the work can be hard but in the end we usually stronger because of the struggle. The next time you are faced with a difficult situation, you should not allow it to control you; rather you should be the one to take control of the situation and power through. You'll be grateful that you did.

The first in overcoming any obstacle is to acknowledge your emotions. Choosing to ignore them is the equivalent of trying to run away from the problem that is right in front of you. The only successful way to overcome them is to stop, and examine the emotions you are feeling. If you choose to wallow in the pain of the moment, or replay events over and over in your mind, you are not allowing yourself to feel the loss, pain, anger, and sadness that is present. You should also not try to rationalize your feelings; instead you should accept them as part of the journey that you are currently on.

It is also important that you not bottle up your feelings when faced with a challenge. When you keep your emotions locked up inside, you are only allowing them to become worse and result in a higher level of anxiety. Talking about what is currently going on in your life will allow you to better understand how it is affecting you. You can also gain valuable insight from those around you who may have gone through the same experience at some point. They found the strength to power through and so can you.

When you are experiencing a crisis, it may be difficult for you to see any positive side of the situation. However, if you can give yourself some distance from the situation you may be able to see things from another perspective. The situation you are currently in does not have to be permanent, you have the ability to overcome it and step through to the other side. It may not happen overnight, but if you allow yourself the proper amount of time and do the necessary work, you will realize that you can overcome it.

When we experience a stressful situation or are faced with what seem to unsurmountable obstacles, we can't allow them to control every aspect of our life. It is still important that we continue to carry on with the healthy habits we have developed. If your body is strong, it can then help your mind accept the situation and develop a plan to overcome it. Now is not the time to let your body become weak, you're going to need all of the strength you have to successfully power through any difficult situation you are faced with.

Write down the difficult situations you have ahead of and different ways you can approach them to solve them.

_____

_____

_____

_____

_____

_____

_____

_____

_____

_____

_____

CHAPTER 25

PUSH ON

If you're ready to move forward in your life and stop dwelling on things that keep you weighed down, there is no better time than right now. While this may not be as easy as it sounds, if you're truly ready to push on and accept that life has better things waiting for you, you can do it. Starting right now, all you have to do is acknowledge that you are ready. After that, you can then begin the necessary work you need to do in order to push on and move into a different stage of your life.

One of the first things that you should let go of is the importance that you place on the opinions of others when it comes to your life. People may think they know who you truly are, but when it comes down to it, you are the only one who knows your story. They may be familiar with what you have done, whether it was good or bad, but they do not know or understand what you've been through. They base their opinions on what they think they know which is why you should not give those opinions power to control your current life or your future.

The next thing that you need to let go in order to push on is the guilt or shame of the past. We have all experienced some type of failure at some point. We need to accept that it's okay to fail. Failure is what helps us push on the right solution. Your past does not define your future, your future is a blank book and you are the only one who can write the story. Simply because you have failed in the past, does not have any relevance on your current situation. Push on from the fear of failure and accept that it is just another part of life.

The ability to make a decision and stick to it can be another reason why you are unable to push on. You will never be able to leave where you currently are if you cannot make a decision on where you would rather be. When you find and discover what you truly are passionate about, it will become much easier for you to push on from where you currently are and follow your passion. You may notice that prior to realizing what you are truly passionate about, you may have lacked a significant level of drive and success. This is because you were unfulfilled with your situation and the work you were doing. Once you find out what you are passionate about, you will have more energy, become more productive, and look forward to each new day.

Finally, in order to push on and lead a happier and more fulfilling life, you need to learn how to appreciate the present. We spend so much time focusing on the past and the future that we tend to overlook what is happening right now. When we do this, we often fail to realize that the happiest times of our lives are not the accomplishments that we have spent years striving for, but the little moments that happened along the way. Take the time to cherish the now rather than the past or future. If you do, you will be able to push on and create the type of life you have always wanted.

Ask yourself - What Is Holding Me Back? Am I Living In The Present? Am I Indecisive? How Can I Live More In The Present?

CHAPTER 26

THE IMPORTANCE OF BALANCE IN YOUR LIFE

Think of a teeter totter. When matched with the right partner you can enjoy hours of fun – when not matched with the right partner you can be the one stuck doing all the work or the one going for a free ride. A good balance brings harmony to any situation and a valuable key for anyone looking to change. Without balance you will either burn out or under achieve.

The law of reciprocity states, "For every action there is an equal or opposite reaction." Do not let excess become a habit. Learn to live with moderation. Use your funds for life improvement, positive experiences, and helping people. This way you will be sowing good seeds and keeping harmony in your path.

Consider balance as a tool to apply to any application that you may be working on. If you are looking for wealth, then apply balance as you receive it. If you earn or receive a considerable amount of money, give some to help other deserving people. This action justifies your initial focus, because you are having a positive effect on others and sowing good seeds. The cycle will then continue.

Think of balance as it applies to your body, so you can enjoy a healthy life. Try to eat a balanced diet and exercise in a balanced way. In most cases when something goes wrong, it is because balance has been disrupted. This is especially true with illness. Disease will manifest when the body has lost its natural balance.

BALANCE AFFIRMATIONS

It is easy making the necessary corrections in my life, and it is easy for me to make them and keep in balance.

I know exactly what to do and how to do it to manifest what I want in my life, easily and effortlessly, in divine order and balance with all things.

I always learn and take something positive from every situation, therefore I never fail, and I stay in balance.

I am never quick to make judgment.

I am always prepared to listen.

I communicate easily and negotiate what I believe is right for everyone.

Through the Power of my Creator, I have total knowledge and abundance at my disposal.

I eat wholesome foods and drink plenty of water; this keeps my systems in balance.

I sleep peacefully every night as my body recharges its systems.

I take time to breathe deeply and fully and this gives me great energy and brings balance to my life.

I live each day with commitment, purpose, power, and balance.

I am now enjoying and experiencing financial balance in my life.

Remember to strive for balance in everything you do, because once you understand balance, you will achieve happiness. Can you think of a time where your life was off balance? What was the trigger? Do you know exactly what part of your being it was that lost the balance – mind, body, soul? What steps did you take to get back on track?

_____

_____

_____

_____

_____

CHAPTER 27

THE IMPORTANCE OF RECIPROCITY IN YOUR LIFE

If you understand the law of reciprocity then you understand life. When you understand life then you have become a developed spirit. The life of a developed spirit is one worth celebrating.

Although there are different kinds of karma, they are all based on the principle, "For every cause there will be an effect and for every effect there will have been a cause." The Law of Reciprocity rings true. The ground can only give to you what you give to the ground. If you sow good seed, you will reap good seed. If you sow bad seed, you will reap bad seed.

Hence, generosity is an important part of life. Scripture reminds us to give and it will be given back to us. Look at any situation, be it personal, global, or spiritual, and you will see that it's a result of generosity or the lack thereof. It then follows, if you sow good seed in everything you do, you will know happiness quickly. From the very moment that you understand and live by this principle, you will see dramatic and positive change. This may seem easy, but it isn't. If it were easy then we would all be living on some higher place of existence far removed from the material world.

We have all lived many lives, some well and some not so well. They were all a part of a grand unfolding drama of cause and effect. With each lifetime, your spirit grew and developed and now you find yourself reading these words. Can it all be just a coincidence or is it something far more profound?

As human beings we tend to make life quite complicated, even though it really doesn't need to be. By understanding the law of reciprocity and being conscious of our actions and how they affect us, we can control our growth and development, thereby creating the kind of lives we want. Peace and happiness are yours when you truly utilize the law of reciprocity for everyone's best interest.

GENEROSITY AND RECIPROCITY AFFIRMATION

I show compassion and patience in all that I do.

The more I have, the more I give.

I can have anything that I truly desire, if it is for my best interest.

I always say the right thing at the right time.

I complete all that I start easily and enjoyably.

Every day and in every way, things improve for me.

I help and treat others as I would myself.

I enjoy myself today and have fun with everything I do.

I don't have problems, just opportunities.

Everything that comes to me is for my best interest and highest good.

The creation of new reciprocity is ongoing. Everything you do, how you react, how you think, and how you feel dictate the type of new reciprocity and energy you create. It's probably one of the single most important things you do.

Ask yourself - What am I most grateful for? How often do I thank others? How often do I verbally thank myself? What does giving thanks look and feel like to me?

_____

_____

_____

_____

CHAPTER 28

THE IMPORTANCE OF EXPRESSING GRATITUDE EACH DAY

Today, work to draw inward to improve your outer life. As you meditate, extend gratitude for silence. Silence is productive; it causes you to evaluate your outer life and make enhancements. Your tactic with any problem should focus on input and output to your brain. Your brain has connections, neural networks, and patterns of activity for every conditioned habit you experience, whether it's physical or emotional. Practice putting out positive energy in every space you occupy by first controlling your thoughts and language. After all, gratitude is a muscle. Let's exercise it!

Practicing gratitude does not have to be a challenge, but it will take increased awareness & effort. It is the exercise of seeing the quality of things alongside the quantity. It is both, subconscious and conscious assessment you place on people, events, and challenges in your life. It truly boils down to this: Despite how these things affect you, you're ultimately responsible for determining to what extent that affect takes place. Does it remain superficial, or does it change the essence of your being? Understanding this, employ these three techniques to find gratitude in things:

Accept & Reflect - At the core of gratitude is acceptance. Accept what transpires in your life and reflect on it. If it was positive, understand that those who have been given much – much should be given. Remain humble. If it was negative, understand that in every awful thing is a lesson, like a beacon of light that can correct all future paths. Remain open-minded and positive.

Use Mantras - Repeat specific words and positive phrases with intentionality. This will keep your mind in a positive place. When you begin to change your language, your life literally changes! Repeat these when you need that extra thoughtfulness.

- *I appreciate abundance in my life and I allow myself to expand in gratitude, success, and joy every day.*

- *Gratitude brings me into a harmonious relationship with the good in everyone and everything that surrounds me.*

- *Thank You (While this is simple, it is very powerful).*

Truly Be Grateful, One With Experience - Finally, in order to truly reach a place of gratitude, you must truly seek it. We often find ourselves desiring things that we do not actually want or need, and this can affect us when seeking gratitude. Once you understand that you and your experience are one, you realize that whatever has happened, good or bad is simply part of what is. This brings us back to acceptance, and ultimately, gratitude.

Extending gratitude for the past can positively affect your future. Research has shown that people who think about the past in an optimistic way have increased capacity for happiness. If you have bad memories, you might be able to change them to neutral or good feelings by challenging your thinking or through forgiveness. This means that you have ultimate control over your feelings about the past. If you can control your thoughts and language, you can influence your happiness level. This might not be easy at first. It takes practice. Use this mantra to help, "My past does not dictate my future. I extend gratitude for those past experiences because they are shaping me daily."

Incorporate Gratitude into the fabric of your daily life. Controlled experiments have shown that people who record things they're grateful for experience an increase in joy, happiness and overall satisfaction with their lives. Keep a journal of those things you are grateful for. This is because when you focus on things you're grateful for, you amplify good memories about the past. Keep at it!

Challenge your negative thoughts about the past. This can be helpful. By challenging these memories, you might realize that the way you think about the event is not actually "correct" or accurate, and that this faulty thinking is making you feel negatively about something that actually deserves neutral or even positive feelings.

Give gratitude for even those negative experiences you have in your life. With every negative there is a positive yet without the negative you may have never had the positive encounter. You might be experiencing a whole lot of thoughts and feelings about the past. Once you identify negative feelings about the past, challenge them. Extend gratitude for those feelings, events, and even people. Then, see if you can re-write your history and even more so re-create how you view those experiences. Remember that the way you think about the past will influence the way you feel about it, and you can control this! It's simple, EXTEND GRATITUDE!

The intentional use of positive language through expressing gratitude is about "BEING AWAKE" to life. Changing your language requires awareness & intentionality. Conscious intentions hold the key to life change. While expressing gratitude is both subconscious and conscious, I believe it requires much more awareness than we care to give. You are the Creator and your life in fulfillment is the work of art. Extending gratitude is truly fulfillment for the soul. Life isn't simply about getting the things you want...but more so about aligning yourself to put out all that you expect to receive. Align your language by practicing gratitude and you will unlock unlimited possibilities.

Don't just say Thank You, FEEL IT. The only secret to infinite abundance in your life is praying divine prayers of Gratitude. Nothing in life comes to manifestation without Gratitude. When you hear gratitude, it is not about just saying, "Thank You" instead you must FEEL IT!

How do you feel it? You feel it through committing genuine random acts of kindness. Your soul should be magnetizing as you extend gratitude. You should feel internal increase as you practice giving with authenticity. Today, commit to making a phone call and sharing your heart with someone you have not talked with in a while. Tell them how much you give gratitude for them.

Start a personal Pay it Forward campaign – List 5 people to start with that this month you will do something nice for with no reason other than just to be nice.

_____

_____

_____

_____

_____

_____

_____

_____

_____

_____

_____

_____

_____

_____

_____

_____

_____

_____

_____

_____

CHAPTER 29

LAUGHTER VERSUS ANGER

"Laughter is a language that feeds your soul." ~*Jotina Buck*

As teenagers, we did as much as possible to blend in with the crowd. If we can just fit in, then we wouldn't get picked on, and we wouldn't become a target. Now as adults we have to decide whether or not we will celebrate who we are.

If we're embarrassed about our unique characteristics, then we're simply going to try to blend in again. Or, we're going to try to buy new characteristics that will make us into better people. Certainly, the new version of us will be more appealing, right? But how many times do we have to reinvent ourselves before we find a version that we're pleased with?

We already possess characteristics and quirks worth celebrating. What if we were simply grateful for whom we already are? We could focus more on sharing those quirky characteristics to help enrich the world.

I've been on a big kick lately to examine what I can uniquely bring to my work environment, to my family, and to groups I'm a part of. By focusing on what I'm uniquely suited for, I allow room for others to contribute their unique gifts. I can not only celebrate who I am but who they are, as well.

Today, take a moment to consider what characteristics and quirks you can celebrate and be grateful for. Then, rock them out. Look for ways to highlight those characteristics, to be you times 10! You are fearfully and wonderfully made. Extend gratitude for simply being YOU!

Get yourself a desk calendar with a new cartoon every day, share a joke you got via e-mail, tell a co-worker the cute thing your kid said or talk about the funny scene in the latest hit movie. These simple practices will lower your blood pressure, calm your pulse and generally help you release a lot of stress.

"Holding on to anger is like grasping a hot coal with the intent of throwing it at someone else; you are the one who gets burned." - Buddha

Gratitude just can't coexist with anger. You can't be angry and grateful at the same time. Anger, whether it's expressed aggressively, defensively, or passively, should be considered a fear-based emotion. People become angry when they feel threatened: as when an enemy is coming against them. It's just not possible to be aggressive and submissive at the same time. Likewise, it's not possible to be angry and grateful at the same time.

Which emotion has to yield? Which emotion takes precedence?

It is vitally important for you to understand that your "frequency" has everything to do with manifestation. Feelings like anxiety, depression, anger and resentment have a low frequency, while gratitude, love, excitement and joy have a high frequency. We connect with Spirit only in a high frequency. The manifestation gurus state that manifesting results from repeatedly visualizing what you want with positive emotion. I know this to be true from my own personal experience.

Gratitude is one of the most positive emotions we have. Start today to move out of the negative circle of focusing with anxiety and resentment on what you don't have and instead focus on what you do have and what you want with gratitude, excitement and joy! It may well be "more blessed to give than to receive," but also note that it's more powerful.

"For every minute you are angry you lose sixty seconds of happiness."
~Ralph Waldo Emerson

Your mental state is grows stronger with the practice you are put in. As the old saying goes, "practice makes perfect." Keep at it. You are building mental toughness and discipline. You should notice by now that expressing gratitude is becoming a part of your daily language. This characteristic should be at the top of your arsenal of responses to negative stimuli.

In positive psychology research, gratitude is strongly and consistently associated with greater happiness. Gratitude helps people feel more positive emotions, relish good experiences, improve their health, deal with adversity, and build strong relationships. Just like any other skills we must nourish and nurture gratitude.

Why Cultivating Gratitude is Essential
Gratitude allows us to celebrate the present.
Gratitude magnifies positive emotions.
Gratitude blocks toxic, negative emotions.
Grateful people are more stress resistant.
Grateful people have a higher sense of self-worth.

Finally, I think it's important to think outside of the box when it comes to gratitude. Mother Theresa talked about how grateful she was to the people she was helping, the sick and dying in the slums of Calcutta, because they enabled her to grow and deepen her spirituality. That's a very different way of thinking about gratitude. Extend gratitude for what we can give as opposed to what we receive. This can be a very powerful way of cultivating a sense of gratitude.

Your habits, your relationships, your environment, and especially what you think about them have a huge impact. As an aspiring therapist, I know that those things determine more about how happy you are than your genes do, because I've watched so many people learn how happiness works.

When you look at your own behavior, thoughts and feelings more objectively, you can change the things that are subtracting from your happiness. My personal suggestion is focus on gratitude, and work to increase the positive factors in their lives, and decrease the negative ones.

You can improve every area of your happiness: your relationship with yourself, your relationships with others, your work life, your home life, and even your health. While you're at it, take a little time to congratulate yourself on your personal pursuit of happiness, because Celebration + Appreciation = Motivation. The more you understand that increasing your happiness is working, the more motivated you will be to do more, and be even happier.

As you discover the techniques that are most effective for you, make a little reminder note about the best ones. Keep it handy, so if your happiness level starts to slide, you can bring it back up to where you want it. And have a happy life!

There are three things you can do to bring more happiness into your life:

1. Gratitude: Remember to notice and be thankful for whatever you have, what your friends, family and partner do for and give to you.

2. Generosity: Giving to others, especially giving thanks and kindness, will make you happy because most others will give back.

3. Ethics: Living your life according to a set of ethics that make sense to you will make you feel good about yourself, and increase your happiness.

Today, practice these techniques shared and be sure to journal about your experience.

Repeat after me, "God got me no matter what!" Some days you must remind yourself who's on your team and who's fighting for you. Joshua 1:9 says... "Be strong and courageous; do not be afraid because God is with you wherever you go." He is Immanuel! God with us. Today, rest in knowing that all things concerning you are equally important to Our Father!

_____

_____

_____

_____

CHAPTER 30
ACCEPT THAT GOD IS IN CONTROL

I can finally admit I've been a pretty controlling person all my life. Don't blame me! It's my parent's and sibling's fault! LOL…After all, I am the baby of my family and a sad face often times got results. Well, I have learned over time and the hard way that a sad face with God doesn't really work. He does things when He wants and how He wants. Many times in the past I've lost hope and peace because everything looked the same month after month and things were not happening on MY TIME.

The more I journey with God the more liberated I become to "JUST BE" and allow Him to be in Control! I am convinced that if we could really see how God is orchestrating everything behind the scenes, we wouldn't worry. I believe with my whole heart that God has a bright prearranged future for each of you. Use your spiritual imagination to peer into the unseen realm and see God working things out in your favor!

Release control and dismiss the daunting questions…How am I going to get through this problem? Why won't my dream come to past? How can I change my child? When am I going to get married?

Instead say, "Father, I trust you. I believe you are in complete control. And even though I may not see anything tangible happening, I believe you are working in my life, going before me, making crooked places straight, and causing me to be at the right place at the right time. I release total control to you and I embrace peace."

Have you ever seen a magician at work? Many times they use a phrase like "hocus pocus" or "abracadabra" while performing their tricks. Words are associated with manifestation and magic. While pulling a rabbit out of a hat doesn't seem like much, those words serve as a signal to grab your attention. They alert you to an upcoming change or transformation.

Watching your language is very important as words contain a great deal of power. They can be used to help or hurt and have the power to persuade. You can even use words to help you live a more positive life!

The same goes for incantations, spells and prayers. While they appear to be mere statements, those words pack a big punch. Those words coupled with intention, serve as vibrations that carry forth out into the Universe for manifestation. As the Bible says "ask and you shall receive." Words are powerful transmitters.

Most of us have personally experienced the power of words within our own lives. Haven't you been affected by someone's words at some point? Maybe you were encouraged by a friend's kind words or hurt by the words of a lover. Either way, those words had an impact on your life. Write down times when others have said something to you that had a negative impact on your being. Now write down times when people have spoken words that have had a [positive impact on you. Go back and cross out all of the negative statements and highlight only the positives. Only keep those positive statements in your memory databank. The negative does not serve you.

_____

_____

_____

_____

_____

_____

_____

CONCLUSION: MAKE YOUR MESS YOUR MESSAGE

A few months ago I was watching the ESPY Awards and was inspired by a young lady who had experienced trauma after some of her greatest accomplishments. She had sought out all her life to become a great sports journalist. During her era, a woman becoming a sports journalist was unheard of but she was determined. She landed a job with ESPN and from there she began to soar. About 15 years into her career she transitioned from sports journalist to one of prime time television morning broadcasts, Good Morning America. While she had then exceeded her lifetime goal and was soaring high...she received the news that would knock her down off her pedestal. This woman was told she had breast cancer. And before the nation Robin Roberts fought cancer. She agreed to allow a camera crew to follow her journey may it be good or bad. She'd periodically appeared on Good Morning America. She worked while showing the world what courage looked like. Unbeknownst to the world, in her private time she struggled with the, "WHY ME's"? After going into remission and celebrating, Robin received more devastating news. The treatment had given her a blood disease that required her to have a bone marrow transplant and to be quarantined. During this time her mother was also gravely ill. Robin went to her mother's side to be with her during her finals days and hours, and held her hand as she took her last breath. Keep in mind, the world was watching. Many asked Robin why she allowed the cameras to follow her through such a traumatic and private experience - Robin said, "My mom always taught me to Make my Mess my Message."

I gain great inspiration in Robin Robert's message and her story resonates in my heart. I want to echo the sentiments of Robin's mother, "MAKE YOUR

MESS YOUR MESSAGE!"

How to make your mess your message? You must have courage to face your past. You may be asking, "What does my past have to do with where I currently am?" Often times in life we find ourselves in places where we've made a mess too big to bear. We are often haunted by our past and secrets. We try our best to suppress it. Life has dealt us a few tough blows and essentially knocked us down. Being the humans we are we find ourselves saying, "Oh I'm okay! It'll be better tomorrow." When our friends or family ask us how we're doing. We quickly say, "Oh I'm great, I'm blessed and highly favored." Y'all know how we do. We want to quickly rush through those conversations so we can simply get on with our life already. We internalize the mess or state we're in and in some cases sink into a fatal state of depression, anxiety, or stress.

Please understand...Your past is a part of who you are and who you will become. But you'll never be able to fully share the message without first facing your past

You must have Courage to Tell the Story...

Once you've faced your past, don't be afraid to tell the story. Yes it is scary and can be a bit overwhelming but somebody out there is waiting on you and your story. The things we experience in life are not meant for us to keep to ourselves. God's glory is wrapped up in your story. His glory is waiting to be revealed. There's healing in your story, there's increased faith in your story, there's revelation in that story, there's wholeness in that story! And ultimately there's help for someone else in your story. Without sharing your message others may not be delivered from their own mess. I know it is scary to share your story and share with people where you been and even in some cases where you currently are. But the bible tells us that we are overcome by the words of our testimony (Revelation 12:11). Have the courage to tell the story.

You must have Courage to Celebrate your Future...

Lastly you must have the courage to celebrate your future. I know people will think you're crazy or have completely lost your mind. Don't worry, your future is bright. There is greater ahead. No, it may not look like it now because you may still be dealing with some mess, but be of good courage and faith and know God is prepared to deliver you to a place of greater. Starting today begin to speak positive affirmations about your life and your future. Take care of you. Cherish your growth.

CHANGE YOUR LANGUAGE, CHANGE YOUR LIFE PARTNERS

Thanks to every business listed for partnering with Jotina Buck, author of Change Your Language, Change Your Life. Thanks for your investment. I give the highest recommendation for each company listed.

Chef CJ's Masterpiece
Clinton Douglas
www.cjaworkofart.wix.com/cjsmasterpiece

DJ Indurance
Tron
djindurance@gmail.com

Natty's Cakes
LaCharra Henderson
naterycakes@gmail.com

Get Launched Business Development Services
Christy Staples
christy@getlaunchedtoday.com

K'Smith Photography
Karenda Smith
h11productioncompany.com
ksmithqos@gmail.com

D'Concierge Wedding Planning
Darryl Wilson, Jr.
www.dconcierge.net
dwilson@dconcierge.net

Naturally Happy Hair
Crystal L. Knight
Naturally Happy Hair Magazine
cknight@naturallyhappyhair.com
www.naturallyhappyhair.com

Great Minds Think Alike
Dr. Sonya Sloan
www.MotivateandEmpowerWomen.org
MEWE@MotivateandEmpowerWomen.org
1.855.234-MEWE (6393)

BNB Consulting
Ramone & Verily Harper
bnbconcultingllc.com
info@bnbconsultingllc.com

Brian Keith Productions
Brian Keith
briankeithproductions.com
info@briankeithproductions.com

I AM COMMITTED TO YOUR LIFE CHANGE THROUGH POSITIVE LANGUAGE

Thank you for the opportunity to share the wisdom and enlightenment I have gained through my life's journey, my studies, and my Life-Changing practice with you. I sincerely pray that you will put everything you have learned into practice in your life right away. I am committed to your life change through positive language. I am passionate about ensuring a creative approach to create change and produce sustainability through positive language.

I look forward to connecting with each of you. Please feel free to email me at info@jotinabuck.com to share your experience with reading this book. I personally read each email message, and I look forward to hearing your success stories.

Zig Ziglar said, "People often say that motivation doesn't last. Well, neither does bathing — that's why we recommend it daily." Keep speaking life DAILY! I send newsletters with new **Change Your Language, Change Your Life Keys to Unlock Unlimited Possibilities**, so please visit www.jotinabuck.com to join my subscriber list. I look forward to writing to you and helping you explore creative approaches to create the life you desire.

For more information on how to take advantage of my different life changing programs directly with me, visit **www.jotinabuck.com** to learn more.

To book a speaking event for your company, please email **info@jotinabuck. com.** Jotina Buck is the ideal speaker for your next conference, seminar, meeting, or event. Jotina delivers dynamic keynotes and life-enriching seminars for organizations, colleges, universities, youth organizations, corporations and faith-based organizations.

Connect Online:

Visit www.jotinabuck.com
Become Friends at www.facebook.com/JotinaBuck
Follow Jotina at www.twitter.com/jotinab
Connect at www.linkedin.com/JotinaBuck
Email info@jotinabuck.com